Birds

by Kendrick West

HOUGHTON MIFFLIN HARCOURT
School Publishers

PHOTOGRAPHY CREDITS: Cover © SBP/Alamy; 1 © ARCO/D. Usher/age Fotostock; 2 © Blickwinkel/Alamy; 3 © Martin Fowler/Alamy; 4 © Mark Duffy/Alamy; 5 © Wiz Data, Inc./Alamy; 6 © Konrad Wothe/Minden Pictures; 7 © ARCO/D. Usher/age Fotostock; 8 © SBP/Alamy; 9 © Blickwinkel/Alamy; 10 © Wim Weenink/Foto Natural/ Minden Picture

Printed in China

ISBN-13: 978-0-547-42734-8
ISBN-10: 0-547-42734-4

3 4 5 6 7 8 0940 18 17 16 15 14 13 12 11 10

Look at the birds.
They will have baby
birds soon.
They will build a nest
to keep the babies safe.

Look at the nest.
The birds use mud
to build their nest.
They may come back to
the nest for many years.

Look at the mother bird.
She lays eggs.
The mother and father
keep the eggs warm **until**
the babies hatch.

Look at the eggs.
An egg begins to move.
A baby bird is inside.
The baby bird cracks
the shell with its beak.

Look at the baby birds.
They are hungry!
The mother and father
catch bugs to feed
their little birds.

Look at all the birds.
They sleep in the nest
at night.
There may be eight
birds in a nest.

The mother bird calls for help if she sees danger. Other birds come to help. They come to help keep the babies safe.

Look at the little birds.
Now they have feathers.
They are learning to fly!
They follow each other
from tree to tree.

Look at the young birds.
They are ready
to fly away!
Soon they will build
their own nests.

Responding

Word Builder

What do baby birds need to grow?

Talk About It

Text to Text Think of another story about baby animals. How are baby birds different from other baby animals?

baby
begins
eight
follow
learning
until
years
young

Picture what is happening as you read.